Makers as INNOVATORS JUNIOR

Remixing Toys

By Pamela Williams

Published in the United States of America by
Cherry Lake Publishing
Ann Arbor, Michigan
www.cherrylakepublishing.com

Series Editor: Kristin Fontichiaro
Reading Adviser: Marla Conn, MD, Ed., Literacy Specialist,
Read-Ability, Inc.
Photo Credits: All photos by Pamela Williams

Library of Congress Cataloging-in-Publication Data has been filed and is available
at catalog.loc.gov

Cherry Lake Publishing would like to acknowledge the work of the Partnership for
21st Century Learning. Please visit *www.p21.org* for more information.

Printed in the United States of America
Corporate Graphics

A Note to Adults: Please review the instructions for the activities in this book before allowing children to do them. Be sure to help them with any activities you do not think they can safely complete on their own.

A Note to Kids: Be sure to ask an adult for help with these activities when you need it. Always put your safety first!

Table of Contents

Things your parents played with as children can be just as fun as today's toys.

A New Way to Play

Do you have a favorite toy? Your toy may be special to you for a number of reasons. Maybe it moves, makes noise, or lights up. You would probably be disappointed if this favorite toy broke. But if it does, don't throw it away just yet. You can have a lot of fun with a broken toy!

Have you ever wondered what was inside a toy? Why not open one up and see?

Inside a Toy

One way of finding out how something works is by taking it apart. When you take a toy apart, you might be surprised at what you find inside. You might find out why a broken toy is not working. You might even be able to fix it! If not, you can **disassemble** the toy and use its parts to create something new.

Toy Tools

You will need tools to help you take toys apart. Some tools may be sharp and can be hard to use. Always wear protective goggles over your eyes and ask an adult for help. Tools that might be helpful include screwdrivers, scissors, and pliers.

Toy remixing requires using your imagination. It is a fun way to express your creativity.

From Old to New

Using parts of broken toys to create a new toy is called remixing. Toy remixing is a great way to reuse broken or unwanted toys. It is lots of fun, too! You get to create new toys while learning about science and **technology**. You also get to show off your creativity.

Start with a collection of interesting toys to use in your toy remixing.

Choosing Your Toys

The first step is to collect some toys you can take apart. Tell your friends and family that you are collecting broken toys. You can also find old, inexpensive toys at resale shops and garage sales. Be sure an adult knows your plans before you take any toy apart.

The Many Parts of a Toy

Some interesting toys to take apart are those that move or make noise. When you open them up, you may see all kinds of interesting pieces inside. Look for familiar technology such as lights, speakers, and **circuit boards**.

Collect your tools ahead of time. Some tools need adult supervision. Remember to follow safety rules when using them.

Take a Toy Apart

Look carefully at the toys you've collected. Try to figure out how they are put together. Look for screws, buttons, or other things that you can remove or open. Next, gather the tools that will help you take the toys apart. Be sure to ask an adult for help if you need it. Once you have disassembled the toys, lay all the pieces out in front of you.

Toy remixing combines the best of your favorite broken toys.

Creative Decisions

Now it's time to decide which parts to mix. You might choose to mix the toys so they look funny. Or maybe you'd rather build a toy that does something interesting. Try using some of the technology you found in the toys in a new way.

Asking Questions

When deciding how to mix toy parts, ask yourself a few questions. Which toy pieces do you like best? Which parts would mix best with others? Can the pieces easily fit together? If not, how can you attach them to each other? These questions will help you imagine the possibilities for your new toy.

Try to combine toys to make interesting new ones.

Putting the Pieces Together

Have you decided what you want to do with your toy parts? If so, you can get started putting your new toy together. Separate the parts you want to use from the other toy pieces. Then figure out which tools you need to attach the pieces together.

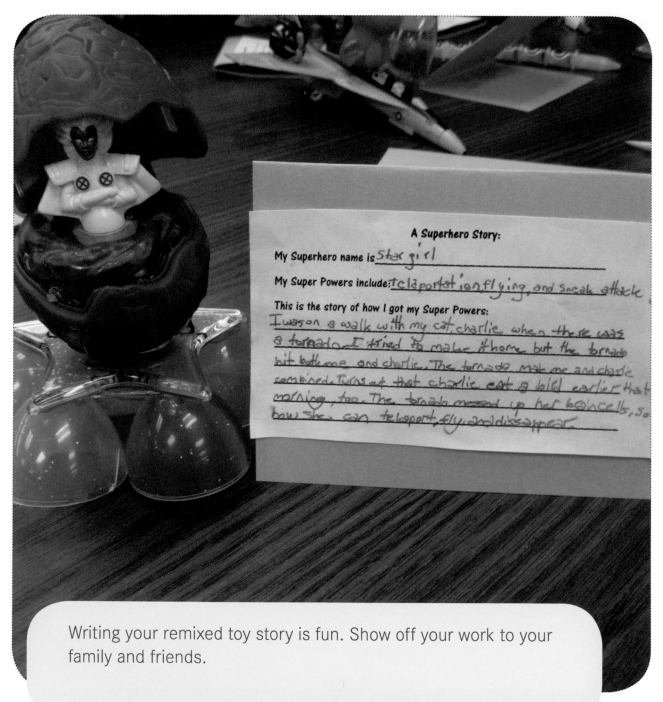

A Superhero Story:

My Superhero name is Star girl

My Super Powers include: tclaportation flying, and sneak attack

This is the story of how I got my Super Powers:

I was on a walk with my cat, charlie when there was a tornado. I tried to make it home but the tornado hit both me and charlie. The tornado made me and charlie combined. Turns out that charlie eat a bird earlier that morning, too. The tornado messed up her brain cells, so now she can teleport, fly, and dissappear.

Writing your remixed toy story is fun. Show off your work to your family and friends.

Your Toy Story

Now you have a remixed toy! It's time to introduce it to the world through storytelling. Write a story about the history of your mixed toy. Is it a hero or a bad guy? How did it come to look like this? Can it do anything cool? You can entertain your friends and inspire them to make new toys of their own!

Upcycling

Using old or broken things to build something new is called **upcycling**. Toy mixing is just one type of upcycling. Can you think of other ways to upcycle everyday objects in your home or at school?

Start your own collection of remixed toys.

Finishing Up

When you are finished, put your tools away. Clean up any mess you made. Organize your toys and toy parts. Be sure to put small pieces in containers. Keep them where you can find them easily. That way you can use them for future projects. Now you are ready to create a remixed toy whenever you get a new idea!

Glossary

circuit boards (SUR-kit BORDZ) pieces of plastic printed with metal pathways that allow electricity to travel through them

disassemble (dis-uh-SEM-buhl) take something apart

technology (tek-NAH-luh-jee) the use of science and math to make things work well and not waste time or energy

upcycling (UHP-syke-ling) the process of using old, broken, or unwanted things in new ways to make them useful again

Find Out More

Books
Fontichiaro, Kristin. *Taking Toys Apart*. Ann Arbor, MI: Cherry Lake Publishing, 2017.

Williams, Pamela. *Starting a Makerspace*. Ann Arbor, MI: Cherry Lake Publishing, 2017.

Web Sites
DIY—Create a Frankentoy
https://diy.org/skills/toymaker/challenges/774/create-a -frankentoy
DIY is a safe online community for kids to discover new passions, level up their skills, and meet fearless geeks just like them. Take a course, post an idea, and get feedback on your DIY (do-it-yourself) projects.

Exploratorium—The Tinkering Studio: Toy Take Apart
https://tinkering.exploratorium.edu/toy-take-apart
Check out some tips for remixing toys and see what other people have created.

Index

About the Author

Pamela Williams is a teacher and a librarian who can upcycle just about anything.